# THE CASTLE ON
# DEVIL'S W[...]

# THE CASTLE ON DEVIL'S WATER

## The Story of Dilston and the Tragic Earl of Derwentwater

Frances Dickinson

The Spredden Press

First published 1969 by the Oriel Press

This edition published 1992 by
The Spredden Press
Stocksfield
Northumberland

© Frances Dickinson 1992

ISBN 1 871739 25 X

Printed and bound by
Smith Settle
Ilkley Road, Otley, West Yorkshire

# CONTENTS

The Right Honourable
James Earl of Derwentwater

G. KNELLER Baron.<sup>t</sup> pinx.          1714.          G. V          sculp.

# INTRODUCTION

Here flowing plenty once did reign,
Which gladden'd ev'ry face;
But now, alas! reversed scene,
*For owls a dwelling place.*

*The Castle on Devil's Water* was first written and published in 1969. Now the book is being republished with a changed format which has enabled me to add much extra material and include additional prints and photographs. Although the central theme remains the same, I have developed the storyline in places where I felt it was appropriate and have provided a family tree which is helpful in unravelling the different generations of Radcliffes and which shows how the direct male line of this large and ancient family had completely died out by the early nineteenth century.

The tragic tale of James Radcliffe and the Jacobite Rebellion has inspired a string of poems, novels and biographies. Although my own interest in the subject was initally aroused by this same romantic and dramatic story, I very soon became equally involved with Dilston itself – a sad, forgotten place, now stripped of all its grandeur, yet still so rich in historical associations. Gradually, a picture of Dilston began to emerge from its beginnings as a busy little township with its baronial castle perched high above the Devil's Water, to the time when it became the home of the rebellious, ambitious Radcliffe family, up until its final days of glory, when James Radcliffe built his grand mansion, Dilston Hall, with its beautiful gardens and grounds stretching down to the river. It is the ruins of this mansion that today are known as Dilston Castle.

Just as this book was about to go to press, I heard that Ingatestone Hall, in Essex, the home of the Petre family (direct descendants of the Radcliffes of Dilston) had opened to the public. It was a great thrill for me to be able to visit the house, to meet Lord Petre and his son, Dominic, and to see for myself the Derwentwater portraits and memorabilia that are exhibited.

For their help and interest in compiling this book I would like to thank: the Reverend Lionel Atherton of Alston for information regarding the Derwentwater clock, the written material being taken from *The Rector and Churchwardens, Alston (Team) Parish* and the photograph of the clock by Dr P. Foreman; Flora Fairbairn of the

Middle March Centre, Hexham, for locating photographs of the death mask, and Ian Foster to whom the photographs belong; Newcastle upon Tyne City Libraries and Arts for permission to reproduce the prints of Dilston Glen and Dilston Mill and the photograph of Dilston Chapel, taken in 1897; Essex Record Office for supplying information regarding the Derwentwater letters and relics; Northumberland Record Office and Ordnance Survey, Southampton, for permission to reproduce the detail from the 1860 Ordnance Survey map; Aidan Cuthbert of Christie's for help in locating certain Derwentwater portraits; Ron Rowland of The National Trust and David Sherlock of English Heritage for their advice on various points; and the Reverend Leonard Constantine of Corbridge for information regarding Dilston Chapel.

I would especially like to thank John and Janet Scholefield, of MENCAP at Dilston Hall, for making me welcome on my many visits and allowing me access to photograph. Here I must add that *the grounds of Dilston are private property and permission to visit must first be obtained from Dilston Hall.*

It is now over twenty years since I first discovered Dilston and was struck by the sorry plight of this beautiful, historic place. However, in the meantime nothing much has changed. Today Dilston still remains Northumberland's forgotten castle. Of course, it is not huge or imposing: in fact, as ruins go, it is fairly modest and unexciting, but the dramatic history and compelling stories that belong to Dilston will, I am sure, continue to intrigue and fascinate all who hear them. I hope that this book will help to draw attention to Dilston and thereby ensure its future preservation.

Frances Dickinson<br>May 1992

# 1. DYVELSTON CASTLE TO DILSTON HALL

A pitiful, deserted ruin is all that remains of the Radcliffe mansion at Dilston in Northumberland. Hidden among trees, high above the banks of the Devil's Water, south-west of Corbridge, these crumbling and forgotten ruins are a pathetic relic of the grand home it used to be. Originally a tower house, of considerable size, it was extensively altered in Elizabethan times. In the following century, a splendid Jacobean extension was added and finally it was enlarged even further to become the imposing eighteenth-century building known as Dilston Hall. Winding downhill from the ruin is a stony track, once a carriageway, which crosses the Devil's Water by a seventeenth-century bridge. The Devil's Water, anciently named the Dyvels or Devels, is a tributary of the Tyne and the settlement that grew up on its banks became known as Dyvelston. This, in turn, became the name of the first family to reside there and throughout the centuries this became abbreviated to Dilston.

The history of Dilston can be traced back to the late eleventh and early twelfth centuries, when it seems that either William II or Henry I bestowed the royal grant upon Aluric of Corbridge and created the barony of Dilston. Aluric was the Chief Officer in Corbridge borough and Sheriff of Northumberland in the reign of Henry I. His son, Richard de Dyvelston, certainly held the barony.

Dilston township originated at this time. It began as an enclosure of the common land in 1296 and was added to at various times.

Of the original thirteenth-century Dyvelston Castle nothing now remains, but its position was located early last century when the examination of a large mound to the west of the present ruin revealed a mass of stonework, consisting of walls six feet thick, chambers and culverts, which had obviously formed part of the old structure. Perched, as it would have been, on the edge of the steep banks above the Devil's Water, this ancient castle must have had a fine, commanding view across the Tyne Valley. The Dyvelston family owned the manor for a few generations until 1317, when Lucy de Dyvelston died leaving no heir and the estate passed to the Tyndales, Lords of the barony of Langley. In the early fifteenth century Dilston again changed hands, this time to the Claxton family, collateral descendants on the female side, and it is thought that the existing tower house was built about 1416 by a William Claxton. The first direct reference to it is in a deed drawn up by Sir

The west front of Dilston Castle, Northumberland

Robert Claxton in 1464. He died in 1484 leaving four daughters and co-heirs, one of whom married a Sir John Cartington. Through their daughter Anne, who married Sir Edward Radcliffe (younger son of Sir Thomas Radcliffe whose father had married a descendant of the ancient family of Derwentwater), the names of Radcliffe and Derwentwater became linked with Dilston. It was to remain the home of the Radcliffe family until the fatal year of 1715. From about 1450, probably for security against invasions of the Scots, the Cumberland Radcliffes had resided at their mansion on Lord's Island, Derwentwater. Set in lovely scenery, this large, convenient house with gardens and orchards continued to be used as a retreat in times of trouble, or sometimes as a summer residence after the family had left Cumberland to live at Dilston.

Sir Edward Radcliffe took up residence at Dilston around the beginning of the sixteenth century and for three generations his family held the office of High Sheriff of Northumberland. It was during this time that the Radcliffes carried out extensive alterations to the old tower house, changing its character and giving it an Elizabethan appearance. The entrance belongs to this time and the stone stairway, directly inside this door, gave access to a second range of buildings to the north, now demolished, as well as leading to floors on four levels. The site of this later extension, with its old hall at ground floor level and great chamber above, can be traced on the north side of the present ruin where brickwork has, at some stage, been added, presumably to prevent the stonework from falling. The two fireplaces which are visible inside the ruin, on the first and second floors, were also added at this time with several mullioned and transomed windows. These windows, though partly restored, are in virtually their sixteenth-century state.

Nothing is left today of the village that once stood on the east side of Dilston Castle, but earthworks can be traced in the fields nearby and Dilston Court Rolls, dating from the beginning of the reign of Elizabeth until 1639, reveal details of life in the busy village community. Tenants were allowed to keep a strict number of sheep on the common, pigs had to be under the charge of a swineherd, but the keeping of goats was strictly prohibited. Some villagers kept hives of bees and weaving was carried out as a cottage industry. Behind the dwellings in the village street were orchards, folds and stackyards. There was a common kiln and bakehouse as well as a common bull for breeding the stock. Regulations and bye-laws were set out and had to be obeyed and upon the village green stood stocks as a warning to evil-doers. Slander was prohibited and bad characters were expelled. Two men were appointed each week to prevent paupers and vagabonds from lodging in the

Dilston Chapel, the gateway to the courtyard of Dilston Hall and the Lord's Bridge were all built in the early seventeenth century by Sir Francis Radcliffe, the first baronet, when he built his Jacobean mansion. Dilston Chapel and the Lord's Bridge were reputed to have been built with money raised for financing the Gunpowder Plot

village. There were restrictions upon tenants regarding the cutting of timber in Dilston woods which were then full of oak, elm, ash, birch, alder and lime. Part of the parkland, called the Roe Park, was stocked with deer.

At the beginning of the seventeenth century the manor of Dilston was owned by Sir Francis Radcliffe who changed the appearance of the existing Elizabethan tower house by adding to it a magnificent mansion which was known as Dilston Hall. This house was, by all accounts, a splendid, timbered, Jacobean structure, with a pillared and battlemented porch, mullioned windows, hall, great chamber, gallery, kitchen and monster chimneys. At the same time alterations were made to the forecourt, enclosing it with an entrance gate to the south, a chapel to the west and other buildings to the east. The latter have since been destroyed, but the chapel and entrance gate still exist, the gate bearing the initials of Sir Francis and his wife, and the date 1616.

It is claimed that the chapel and the Lord's Bridge were built with money raised for financing the Gunpowder Plot. Sir Francis Radcliffe was an ardent Roman Catholic and was accused of being involved in the conspiracy. He was arrested in 1616 but managed to obtain his release and was restored to favour, being created a baronet some years later. Guy Fawkes is reputed to have been at Dilston some time before the plot, using the name of Johnson. For the rest of the seventeenth century, and throughout the Commonwealth years, the Radcliffes, as Catholics, were subjected to repeated fines and penalties for adhering to their faith and refusing to conform to the law of the land.

Sir Edward Radcliffe, the second baronet, was a distinguished Loyalist who fought on the King's side in the Civil War and subsequently suffered forfeiture of his estates, retiring for a while to his residence on Lord's Island in Cumberland. Later, when the trouble had blown over, he returned to Dilston but, in 1645, the mansion on Lord's Island was pillaged and destroyed by Cromwell's men. Sir Francis Radcliffe, the third baronet, managed to retrieve his father's sequestrated estates and, by the end of the century, the rebellious, resourceful Radcliffes had succeeded in acquiring even more land and property, amassing enormous wealth in the process and, finally, in 1688 obtaining an earldom.

In contrast to his ambitious forefathers, Edward Radcliffe, the second Earl of Derwentwater, appears to have had no interest at all in furthering the family fortune. He left the north to live in London where, it seems, he aspired to become a poet. It was not until his son, James Radcliffe, inherited the title of third Earl of Derwentwater and, in 1709, returned from the Continent to live in England, that the Radcliffes

The east front of Dilston Castle. The tower house was built c.1416 and was later incorporated in Dilston Hall. The small windows were added in the sixteenth century while the two large windows on the left were part of the alterations made by James Radcliffe. The forecourt lay in front of this side of the tower with the entrance situated in the central block to the right

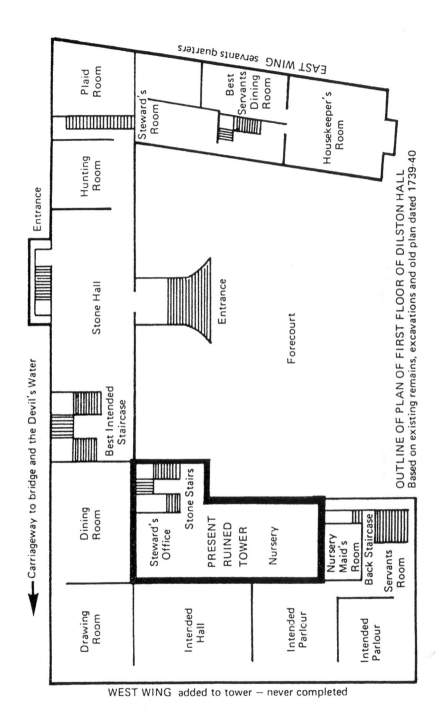

WEST WING added to tower — never completed

Drawing Room

Dining Room

Intended Hall

Steward's Office

Stone Stairs

PRESENT RUINED TOWER

Intended Parlour

Nursery

Nursery Maid's Room

Back Staircase

Servants Room

Intended Parlour

Best Intended Staircase

Stone Hall

Hunting Room

Plaid Room

Entrance

Entrance

Forecourt

← Carriageway to bridge and the Devil's Water

EAST WING servants quarters

Steward's Room

Best Servants Dining Room

Housekeeper's Room

OUTLINE OF PLAN OF FIRST FLOOR OF DILSTON HALL
Based on existing remains, excavations and old plan dated 1739-40

9

began, once again, to take a pride in their family home. Young and aware of fashion, James Radcliffe decided to replace the old Jacobean house with a spacious, modern mansion in keeping with the taste and requirements of the day. Accounts and old prints of this later Dilston Hall show that it was a huge, barrack-like building, with none of the charm of the previous timbered Jacobean house. All that remains of this building today are two large square windows in the eastern wall of the ruin for, after James Radcliffe's execution in 1716, the property fell into disrepair and in 1765 orders were given for its demolition.

Excavations carried out in 1910 and an old plan reveal that the mansion had been built around three sides of a forecourt (see plan), said to have been paved with black limestone, in the middle of which was a fountain, supplied with water from a considerable distance. On the north side of this forecourt, and built on the site of the Jacobean house, was a central block which contained most of the living quarters, the hunting room, and the entrance hall which had once been paved with black-and-white marble with a 'geometrical' staircase at one end. This grand entrance hall was approached from the courtyard by a flight of steps. The eastern wing was mostly servants' quarters with stables and laundries to the north. From under a clock tower at the rear of the mansion, a carriageway led down to the Devil's Water. To the south of the mansion, and separated from it by a roadway, were some enclosed grounds and gardens whose approach was through the gate pillars that stand at the entrance to the grounds of the present house. The fifteenth-century tower house was allowed to remain, being incorporated into the western wing of the new building and adapted for use as a nursery. The western wing was added to the west wall of the tower house, making the block of double thickness. A formal flower garden, with a fountain in the centre, has been traced at this side of the building. This western block was intended to contain the principal reception rooms but never reached completion, for in 1715 the Jacobite Rebellion broke out and on James Radcliffe's departure work was suspended, never to be resumed.

Dilston Chapel stands to the south-west of Dilston Castle. It was built to replace an earlier chapel, dedicated to St Mary Magdalene, that probably stood on the same spot and is referred to in the Patent Rolls of 4 February 1379. It would have served both the castle and little village that clustered around it. The present chapel has the character of a medieval chapel, being lofty in proportion to its width, while the windows are adapted from thirteenth-century work, suggesting that the earlier chapel belonged to this period. The hoodmoulds above the windows date from the renaissance and the doors are Jacobean. At the

Dilston Chapel as it looked in 1897. Ten years after the demolition of Dilston Hall, it was directed that some trees should be planted round the chapel and what remained of the old castle should be preserved when the surrounding grounds were levelled

west end there is a tower, with a staircase which once led up to a gallery where the Radcliffe family were able to worship in private, while the servants and villagers were seated below. The gallery has been removed but marks on the walls outline its position. The shape of a fireplace and a doorway, that once led onto the gallery, are clearly visible on the back wall above the pews. A door on the north side of the tower, which was once the entrance used by the family and servants, has been blocked in, but its position can still be located in the stonework. The door on the south was originally used by villagers. A flight of stone steps at the east end of the chapel leads down to the vault whose entrance is now obscured by rows of pews. On the outside wall, above the east window, are the arms of the Radcliffe family. Built into the wall, below the window, is a Roman gravestone showing the standing figure of a woman. The stone is very weathered and the features are indistinct, but it is probable that the person depicted on the stone was buried near this spot, as the Roman road Dere Street ran close to Dilston. Near to the chapel is a cottage which is believed to have been the residence of the priest.

There are several versions of this view of Dilston Hall. The original was drawn on the spot by Thomas Oliver and published in 1766. Thomas Oliver was an architectural and topographical draughtsman who practised in Hexham around this time. His original drawing was sometimes exhibited at Newcastle in a frame made from wood from the old Tyne bridge

How mournful feeble Nature's tone,
　When Dilston Hall appears:
Where none's to wait the orphan's moan,
　Nor dry the widow's tears!

The helpless aged poor survey,
　This building as it stands;
In moving anguish heard to say,
　(And weeping wring their hands).

The bounteous earl, he is no more,
　Who once adorn'd this plain;
Reliev'd the needy at his door,
　And freely did sustain.

Here flowing plenty once did reign,
　Which gladden'd ev'ry face;
But now, alas! reversed scene,
　For owls a dwelling place.

The tim'rous deer hath left the lawn,
　The oak a victim falls;
The gentle trav'ler sighs when shewn,
　These desolated walls.

Each gen'rous mind emotion feels,
　With pious pity mov'd;
No breast its anguish yet conceals,
　For one so well belov'd.

# 2. HERE FLOWING PLENTY ONCE DID REIGN

The life of James Radcliffe, third Earl of Derwentwater, and the dramatic events of the Jacobite Rebellion which led to his untimely death on the scaffold, must surely rate as one of the most fascinating stories in Northumbrian history.

James Radcliffe was born in Arlington Street, London, in 1689, the eldest of a family of four and a grandson of Charles II. In 1687 his father, Edward Radcliffe, had married Lady Mary Tudor, the illegitimate daughter of the Stuart king and the actress Moll Davis, but the marriage was an unhappy one from the start, eventually ending in separation. This marriage of convenience had been arranged by the ambitious Sir Francis Radcliffe, the third baronet, though Lady Mary was only a girl of fourteen at the time and her husband, Edward, was some twenty years older. Sir Francis had long sought an alliance with the Royal House of Stuart and shortly after the marriage he was created Earl of Derwentwater. After their parents' separation the children of the marriage remained under the guardianship of their father, though they never lived at Dilston as Edward Radcliffe preferred his London home. A second son, Francis, had been born in 1691; another son, Charles, in 1693; and a daughter, Mary, in 1697.

In 1702 James Radcliffe and his brother Francis were sent to France where they were educated and brought up in St Germain at the court of their cousin, the exiled James III. The two boys had been chosen as suitable companions for the young James Stuart by his mother, Queen Mary Beatrice, the widow of James II.

In 1709, at the age of twenty, James Radcliffe received licence to return to England. He had inherited the Derwentwater Estates at his father's death, four years earlier, and upon his return to England he was eager to set out for Dilston, the Northumbrian home he had never seen. So, at the beginning of February 1710, after staying for a short while in London at the home of Dr John Radcliffe, a distant relation, James Radcliffe started on the long journey north. His brother Francis, who had returned to England with him, chose to remain in London, for the idea of living in the wild, uncultured north was quite distasteful to him. Francis Radcliffe, it seems, was an irritable, ill-mannered man who suffered from bad health which he felt sure the cold northern climate would not improve.

James Radcliffe liked Dilston at once. It lived up admirably to all that he had heard and he immediately began to make enthusiastic plans for the improvement and comfort of his new home. As preparations for his arrival were still being made at Dilston he stayed for a while with Thomas Errington at Beaufront, on the opposite bank of the Tyne, where he became acquainted with the various neighbouring families. His arrival must have caused considerable excitement for he was rich, fashionable and sociable, and in every possible way a very eligible bachelor. He soon became popular among the northern people for his kind heart, courteous manner and open-handed hospitality, which endeared him to all, whether humble tenants or rich neighbours. Because of his Catholic upbringing with his cousin, James Stuart, some had feared that he might try to force his religious beliefs upon them, but all fears were quite unfounded for James Radcliffe had no such intentions and treated both Catholics and Protestants in the same charitable way.

Descriptions of the young Earl depict him as being slender and slightly under medium height, with fair hair, grey eyes and a charming smile. The historian, the Reverend Robert Patten, says of him:

> The sweetness of his temper and disposition, in which he had few equals, had so secured him the affection of all his tenants, neighbours, and dependants, that multitudes would have lived and died for him; he was a man formed by nature to be generally beloved; and he had a beneficence so universal that he seemed to live for others. As he lived among his own people, there he spent his estate; and continually did offices of kindness and good neighbourhood to everybody as opportunity offered.

With the young Earl in residence at Dilston, life immediately became busy and lively. Days were spent in hunting, visiting and entertaining with the many friends and relations among the great county families, the Swinburnes, Fenwicks, Erringtons, Collingwoods, Shaftoes, Charltons, Herons, Middletons, Claverings and Forsters. James Radcliffe must have found the rough ways of the Northumbrian gentlemen very different from his own, for his French upbringing had given him an interest in learning and culture that could not be shared with the hard-drinking, sports-loving Northumbrians. But he was always pleasant and courteous and enjoyed entertaining at Dilston, welcoming all in his generous way. His younger brother Charles, then a boy of seventeen, seems also to have been living at Dilston during this time, taking part in the merriment with as much zeal as his elders. Charles Radcliffe was high-spirited and impetuous and was already showing signs of growing into a wild, pleasure-loving gallant.

A particularly close friendship developed between James Radcliffe

*Darnentwater*

*Ann Darnentwater*

*The Third Earl, Countess and heir*

The third Earl, Countess and heir

and his Swinburne cousins at Capheaton, and it seems highly probable that his decision to pull down the old Jacobean house at Dilston and replace it with a mansion, was influenced by the fine new house that had recently been built at Capheaton, designed by Robert Trollope.

In 1712 James Radcliffe married Anna Maria Webb, a Catholic heiress, and under a condition of marriage left the north to live for two years at his wife's father's home at Hatherop in Gloucestershire. Shortly after his marriage he wrote to Lady Swinburne saying:

Dear Cousin, I was married to my great content in every respect on Thursday last. My dear wife, her father and Mother charm me more and more every day, I could wish with all my heart you were a witness of my happiness, and that I had your opinion upon my choice, which if approved of, by so good a judge, would double my pleasure and augment the obligations for ever due to your ladyship from your humble and obedient
servant Derwentwater

While James Radcliffe was away from the north, most of the alterations to the house at Dilston were made and in 1714, when he returned with his wife and young son John, the new mansion was nearing completion. Descriptions of Lady Derwentwater depict her as small and pretty, with dark hair and a lively temperament. She had been educated at a convent school in Hammersmith and was a devoted supporter of the House of Stuart.

During this year Queen Anne died and George of Hanover was immediately brought to England and crowned King. The Jacobites were shocked. They had been certain that James Stuart would cross from France and claim his rightful throne. They could not believe that the people of England would accept a foreigner. But George of Hanover was a Protestant and because of this the people had overlooked all else and welcomed him as their king. They wanted no Roman Catholic to sit on the throne of England. For almost a year messages and plans were exchanged amongst Jacobite sympathizers throughout the north of England and Scotland, and rumours that King James was soon to land filled the air. In July 1715 the first hint of danger disturbed the happy life at Dilston, when it was reported that the Government was passing a law that no Catholic could own a horse worth more than five pounds. James Radcliffe at once sent his most valuable horses, together with his own favourite grey stallion, to a Mr Hunter, a Protestant neighbour, for safety.

Since James Radcliffe's marriage in 1712 his brother Charles had been living mainly in London and had grown wilder and more extravagant

16

than ever. He kept a succession of mistresses, gave them lavish gifts and set them up in richly-appointed houses. His reputation grew and it was whispered all over London that he was taking after his grandfather, Charles II. He was a constant source of worry to James, who was continually paying the debts incurred by his brother. But, despite his reckless nature, Charles was a Radcliffe and was basically honourable, brave and loyal to the Jacobite cause in which he passionately believed. During the troubled summer months of 1715 he returned to Dilston where the air was rife with murmurs of rebellion and James Radcliffe uneasily awaited news of a rising.

Map showing the route taken in the Jacobite Rebellion

# 3. A HOPELESS ENTERPRISE

James Radcliffe took little part in any attempts to organize a rebellion but, because of his position as a Roman Catholic earl and close friendship with the exiled James Stuart, he was immediately under great suspicion. A warrant was issued for his arrest and for several weeks he was forced to live in hiding, sheltering in the houses of friends and cottages of tenants. Shafto Crags, near Capheaton, is reputed to be one of the places where he hid from the authorities, supposedly escaping down a precipitous cliff called Salters Nick. An old Roman altar at Fourstones, near Hexham, is said to be the place where secret letters and messages were passed between the Jacobites, with news of their plans and movements.

Towards the end of September events moved fast. News came that the Earl of Mar had risen with a considerable body of troops in Scotland, and that the Lords Nithsdale, Kenmure and Carnwath, with the Earl of Wintoun, had raised the Stuart standard and were marching south.

It was with great reluctance that James Radcliffe agreed to be party to the Jacobite rising, for his good sense warned him that the rebellion was a hopeless enterprise. However, at the last minute, being persuaded by the enthusiasm of the other Jacobite rebels, including his brother who was impatient to take up arms, he consented to join the rebellion. A traditional story claims that Lady Derwentwater, upset by his apparent lack of spirit, called him a coward and throwing down her fan told him to take it and give her his sword in return. This tale is almost certainly an exaggeration of the facts, for though Lady Derwentwater — like all the other Jacobite ladies — was more enthusiastic about the rebellion than the men, all evidence, including farewell letters from the Earl to his wife, prove them to have been a devoted couple. However, when James Radcliffe, after weeks of hesitation, rode out with the rebels, the Countess was blamed for ever after for her husband's fate.

Tradition holds that the Earl's departure was accompanied by three evil omens. That morning while dressing he lost his treasured Stuart ring, and then, when bidding farewell, his favourite dog howled lamentably and his horse shied and refused to move. James Radcliffe, accompanied by Charles Radcliffe and a small party of servants and neighbours, finally rode out from Dilston to meet the Jacobite forces at Greenrigg on 6 October 1715.

At Greenrigg a small army gathered and Tom Forster of Bamburgh was officially declared General — a disastrous decision, for Tom was a foolish man, of little intelligence and with no knowledge of soldiering. But it was thought that he, a High Anglican Tory, would attract more followers than James Radcliffe, a Roman Catholic earl. From Greenrigg the army marched on to Coquetdale and set up headquarters in Rothbury. Two weeks were spent marching over most of Northumberland where the Jacobites openly proclaimed James III as king. During this time there was little fighting and although in the towns and villages recruits were fewer than had been expected, the Jacobite forces already included members of some of the most prominent families of Northumberland — Widdringtons, Swinburnes, Claverings, Collingwoods, Selbys, Shaftos, Charltons, Erringtons, and others. Among the rebels was the turncoat curate, the Reverend Robert Patten of Allendale, who afterwards wrote *The History of the Late Rebellion*.

News came of the arrival of the Scottish Lowland Lords with their forces under the leadership of William Gordon, Lord Kenmure; and, after proclaiming King James at Warkworth, the army, now about three hundred strong, marched on to Morpeth. The idea was to enter Newcastle where Forster expected to find support, especially among the powerful keelmen. But the first great blow came when on their arrival at Morpeth they heard that Newcastle had declared for King George and had barricaded its gates against them. At the news that a large Hanoverian force had been sent from London under the leadership of General Carpenter, Forster immediately ordered a retreat to Hexham, twenty miles to the west. During this time James Radcliffe had his last glimpse of Dilston, and a quick meeting with his wife and child, before the army was again on the move, heading back to Rothbury.

With still no news of King James sailing from France they agreed to cross the border and make for Kelso, where they were joined by a force of Highlanders under Brigadier-General Macintosh. Now nearly two thousand strong, they made their way towards the border where a dispute arose over whether or not to march into Lancashire. Charles Radcliffe strongly opposed crossing into England, declaring that this would be their ruin, and that unless they could be sure of support in Lancashire it would be wiser to remain in Scotland. He was completely overruled by the other leaders and when the decision to enter England was made over half the Highland force refused to go and deserted. So, with the numbers now reduced to sixteen hundred, the little army crossed the border at Longtown and marched down the west side of the Pennines into Lancashire.

On 9 November the Jacobite army arrived in Preston and proclaimed James III King of England in the market place. The morale of the men

THE WHOLE

# PROCEEDING

## TO

# JUDGMENT

UPON THE

# Articles of Impeachment

OF

# HIGH TREASON

Exhibited by the

Knights, Citizens, and Burgeffes in Parliament Affembled, in the Name of Themfelves and of all the Commons of *Great Britain*, againft *James* Earl of *Derwentwater*, *William* Lord *Widdrington*, *William* Earl of *Nithifdale*, *Robert* Earl of *Carnwath*, *William* Vifcount *Kenmure*, and *William* Lord *Nairn*,

In *Weftminfter-Hall*, on *Thurfday* the Ninth Day of *February*, 1715.

*Publifhed by Order of the Houfe of* PEERS.

*LONDON:*

Printed for *Jacob Tonfon* at *Shakefpear's-Head*, over-againft *Katharine-Street* in the *Strand*. MDCCXVI.

was higher now, for they had been assured on their arrival in the town that King George's regiments were forty miles away and on the run and that the main Government army had been broken up in Scotland by the Earl of Mar. But great was their disappointment when they failed to rally support amongst the Lancastrians, for they had been given to understand that thousands would rise with them in this county and declare themselves for King James.

Three days later came the shattering news that General Wills was marching upon them from Wigan. The Jacobite forces, completely unprepared, hurriedly made attempts to defend the town. Rough barricades were erected in the streets and trenches hastily dug. The dragoons charged the first barricade at two o'clock and from then until evening the battle raged, men, regardless of rank, fighting side by side. With swords and pistols and stripped to their waistcoats James Radcliffe and his brother Charles fought hard and bravely until, as dusk fell, the enemy forces retreated and set up a camp outside the town. But the Battle of Preston was over, for the morning brought the arrival of General Carpenter with reinforcements, and Tom Forster, without any consultation with his colleagues, met the Government generals and agreed to unconditional surrender. Their fate seemed inescapable since the town was completely surrounded. James Radcliffe, together with the other English gentlemen, saw no sensible alternative to surrendering peacefully, but the Highlanders and other Scottish rebels declared that they would rather die fighting than admit defeat. The only English leader to support the Scots was Charles Radcliffe, who bitterly reproached James for his submission and declared fearlessly that 'he would rather die with sword in hand, like a man of honour, than yield to be dragged like a felon to the gallows and be hanged like a dog'.

An attempt to lead the Scots in a charge was promptly crushed and the rebels were assembled, disarmed and formally made prisoner. Sixteen hundred prisoners were taken, among them Lords Derwentwater, Widdrington, Nithsdale, Wintoun, Carnwath, Kenmure, Nairn, and Charles Radcliffe and Charles Murray, as well as members of the Northumbrian families of Collingwood, Thornton, Shaftoe, Errington, Charlton, Riddell, Clavering and Swinburne. Many of the men of humble birth were hanged in Lancashire prisons or transported to American plantations while the leaders, with about two hundred other prisoners, were escorted to London. They entered the city amid shouting, jeering mobs, and, with their hands tied behind their backs, James Radcliffe and the Scottish Lords were conducted to the Tower; while Charles Radcliffe, Tom Forster and about seventy others were taken to Newgate. The Reverend Robert Patten, who had acted as

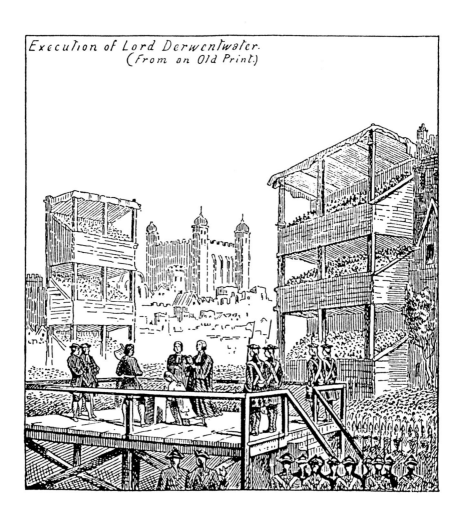

Execution of Lord Derwentwater.
(From an Old Print.)

chaplain during the rebellion, was also sent to Newgate, but, on turning king's evidence to save his own skin, he was released.

James Radcliffe was tried on 9 February 1716 and accused of high treason. Every effort was made to save his life, but even the heart-rending pleas of his wife could not bring King George to show mercy. Together with the other rebel peers he was sentenced to death by beheading, a death which was looked upon as merciful compared with the brutal hanging, drawing and quartering that was the fate of the humbler prisoners. Several of the less distinguished leaders perished at Tyburn and the other noblemen originally accused of treason either received pardons or escaped. Lord Nithsdale escaped on the eve of his execution, so reducing the number of noble victims to two: Lord Derwentwater and Lord Kenmure.

On the night before his execution, James Radcliffe wrote a number of letters to his friends and members of his family. To his wife he wrote:

My Dearest Worldly Treasure,

I have sent you the enclosed, in which is contained all I know, but God knows I have as yet found little advantage by being a plain dealer, but, on the contrary, have always suffered for it, except by my sincerity to you, my dear, for which you made me as happy as this world can afford; and now I offer up the loss I am likely to have of you as a means to procure me eternal happiness, where I pray God we may meet after you have some years exercised your virtues, to the edification of all that know you. I have corrected a few faults in Croft's accounts, but I leave it to you to order everything as you please, for I am morally sure, with the grace of God you will keep your promise. Somebody must take care of my poor brother Charles, to save him if possible. I will recommend him, however by a few circular lines to my acquaintage. Lord Nithsdale has made his escape, upon which our unreasonable governor locked up the gates, and would not let me send the enclosed to you, and immediately locked us all up, though it was not eight of the clock, and could not be my fault, though it may prove my misfortune, by his management. If you do not think the enclosed signifies, make what use you will of it.

Adieu, my dear, dear comfort.

To Charles in Newgate James Radcliffe wrote:

Dear Brother,

You have behaved yourself like a man of honour and bravery . . . God who has been so good to us both by giving us time to repent . . . I have great confidence in His goodness for a merciful forgiveness for us both.

You know, dear brother, we have sometimes disputed together . . . but . . . I believe few brothers would have done more than I would have done to serve you. I have recommended your life . . . to those I know; it may be they will be more successful on your behalf. Pray behave yourself decently and honourably, without pride; bear my death with patience, forgive my enemies as I do; and if ever you are free, live as devoutly as ever you can . .

It is now, dear brother, near the time of execution — God grant me courage to the last. And that we may meet one day in eternal bliss, is the hearty prayer of

Your constant loving Brother,
Derwentwater
Dear Brother adieu

James Radcliffe was escorted to Tower Hill on 24 February 1716 and, wearing a black velvet suit and black plumed hat, ascended the scaffold steps. He was observed to be pale but composed, and when four times he was offered his life if he would conform to the Established Church and accept the House of Hanover he replied, 'Though King James had been of a different religion from mine, I should have done for him all that lay in my power, as my ancestors have done for his predecessors, being thereunto bound by the laws of God and man.'

He died at the age of twenty-seven, displaying such courage and bravery in one so young that he was never to be forgotten. His remains were wrapped in a black cloth and taken to the Tower and were said to have been buried in St Giles-in-the-Fields. Maybe a mock funeral took place for it is certain that the Earl's remains were never buried in London but were surreptitiously removed from the Tower and embalmed, before being taken to Dagenham Park, in Essex, where Lady Derwentwater had stayed during her husband's imprisonment. After resting in a Catholic Chapel for three days they were secretly conveyed to Northumberland, by a little procession that travelled by night and rested by day. On the night of Tuesday 6 March 1716, as the hearse carrying Lord Derwentwater's body was approaching Durham, the entire sky was suddenly lit up by a fiery brilliance, with streamers of flame and colour flashing from east to west. That night, all over England, the *aurora borealis* was brighter than had ever before been known and darkness never came. From miles around people flocked to view the corpse as the crimson pillars of light were said to rise above the hearse and spread from the horizon in the form of an expanded fan. It was fearfully whispered to be an omen of heaven's wrath at the execution of the much-loved Earl and from that time on the Northern Lights became known as 'Lord Derwentwater's Lights'.

The following night the cortège reached Dilston and in candlelight James Radcliffe, third Earl of Derwentwater, was laid to rest with his ancestors in Dilston Chapel. Lady Derwentwater was not present at the burial and never returned to Dilston. A few months after her husband's execution she gave birth to a daughter and went to live at her parents' home in Gloucestershire. The administration of the Derwentwater estates was given to the resident steward and two agents, with whom she corresponded regularly until her death. In 1721 she retired to Brussels with her son and daughter where she lived until 1723 when she died of smallpox at the age of thirty.

Legend claims that the Devil's Water ran red as blood when the gentle young Earl was executed. The probable explanation is the brilliant display of aurora borealis

# 4. THE BOUNTEOUS EARL HE IS NO MORE

The cruel fate of the gentle and beloved Earl of Derwentwater aroused so much sympathy that he became revered as a martyr and superstitions spread rapidly among the peasantry. It was said that the spouts of Dilston ran with blood, and that the corn which was being ground at Dilston mill was tinged with a reddish hue on the day the Earl was beheaded. A poem inscribed on an old print of Dilston Hall expresses the sentiments that were felt among the people.

> Let no unhallow'd tongue, or servile slave,
> Their partial clamour vent beyond the grave;
> But let the noble Dead his honours wear;
> His fault deplore, his virtue still revere:
> Tho' err he did, he finish'd the debate,
> With his own blood, and Radclyffe's fair estate.
> The aged farmer, tott'ring o'er the green,
> Leans on his staff, recounts the days he's seen:
> Informs the list'ning youth by his record,
> How bless'd his roof, how plenteous was his board;
> Nor rack'd by Derwent's hospitable lord.
> He stops his tale, involv'd in grief profound;
> He sighs, he weeps, and feebly strikes the ground;
> Cries, why rehearse these golden days of yore,
> Since they to me, to me can be no more!
> The clement heart, and curious, often calls
> To view the naked park, and stripped walls:
> E'en the damp walls their stony tears impart,
> As if their master's wound had pierc'd their heart.
> Ye pensive mutes, 'tentive on Dilston wait,
> And mourn, eternal Radclyffe's tragic fate!

For a while after the Earl's burial his heart was kept by a surgeon who reported a series of miraculous healings. A woman who had been unable to lift her arm, and several people afflicted with scrofula, were reputedly cured after touching the blessed relic. The heart was eventually taken to France where it was kept by the English nuns at Angers and then removed to the chapel of the Augustine nuns in Paris. It was from here that it disappeared after the chapel was plundered in 1871.

When orders were issued for the demolition of Dilston Hall there was so much sympathy in the neighbourhood for the murdered Earl that obtaining men for the work of destruction was virtually impossible. The job was regarded almost as sacrilegious. Tradition claims that the spirit of the Earl still visits the woods and glades around the Devil's Water, and the apparition of the unhappy Countess is reported to have been seen climbing the stairs of the ruined tower to light the cresset at the top, as she did every night while awaiting her husband's return.

The haunted turret

# 5. A COFFIN FULL OF SAWDUST

Tom Forster, the General of the Jacobite Rebellion, escaped from Newgate with the help of his sister Dorothy a few days before his trial, on 11 April 1716. It is thought likely that the government had turned a blind eye to the escape, in their own interests, as Tom Forster was not a Catholic but a High Anglican Tory. The Forsters had once been a wealthy and powerful family in Northumberland, owning Bamburgh Castle and land in Blanchland. In 1704, after years of excessive spending and riotous living, the family became bankrupt and lost most of their possessions. They were rescued from further embarrassment by Lord Crewe, Bishop of Durham, who had married the aunt of Tom and Dorothy. He bought from the Crown the property the Forsters had held under it and paid off all the outstanding debts. Thereafter, Tom and Dorothy lived at Blanchland in the house that is now The Lord Crewe Arms.

The General of the Jacobite Rebellion

Dorothy Forster, the heroine
of the Jacobite Rebellion

Dorothy Forster became the heroine of the 1715 Jacobite Rebellion when, in snow and ice, she made the long journey from Northumberland to London to rescue her brother Tom from Newgate. The escape was, allegedly, planned and carried out by Dorothy who is said to have bribed the gaoler and, with the help of a blacksmith friend, to have made a set of skeleton keys. In this way Tom Forster fled to France, where he remained until his death in 1738. Immediately after his escape, Dorothy stated that Tom had died in prison and she had an empty coffin placed in the crypt of the church of St Aidan in Bamburgh. Because of this his death is recorded twice, for when he died over twenty years later his body was brought home to Northumberland and placed in the family vault at Bamburgh. Many years later a coffin, filled only with sawdust, was discovered in the chancel where the body was supposed to have been buried, and under it were found two other coffins, one containing the body of Tom Forster and the other that of his sister Dorothy.

# 6. A WILD, COURAGEOUS BROTHER

Charles Radcliffe was put on trial in May 1716. Throughout the entire proceedings his attitude was one of mockery and insolence and, when he was charged with high treason and sentenced to death by hanging, drawing and quartering, he laughed in the Judge's face. Twice during the following months he was reprieved but, doubting that he would ever be fully pardoned, he began to plan his escape. Already several important prisoners had made their escape: Tom Forster was safely in France and, a few days before Charles Radcliffe's trial, Brigadier Macintosh, leading a group of fourteen men, had overpowered the guards in the press-yard and broken out.

Charles Radcliffe escaped from Newgate on 11 December 1716. The higher-class prisoners were occasionally allowed to meet in an upper part of the prison known as the Castle, which was furnished with a few benches and tables, where the prisoners could drink and have entertainment. Weeks of careful investigation and planning had revealed that a small door at the corner of this room led into the debtors' prison where prisoners were allowed considerable freedom and were able to receive visitors. There was frequent coming and going and it was from here that Charles Radcliffe made his escape, simply walking out of Newgate among the visitors, disguised only in a mourning suit and brown tye-wig. For a short while afterwards he resided in London at the home of a female relation, and in December 1716 escaped on a smuggler's vessel to Boulogne.

During the same year the Derwentwater estates were confiscated by the government and held by trustees until 1720 when, following a series of legal battles, they were eventually returned to James Radcliffe's son John, fourth Earl of Derwentwater. However, when John Radcliffe died in 1731 without male issue, the estates reverted to the crown and shortly afterwards, in 1735, they were conferred upon Greenwich Hospital. There have been various conflicting reports of the death of John Radcliffe, but it is generally accepted that he died at the age of nineteen, at his grandfather's home in London, after an unsuccessful operation for the removal of a stone in the kidney. His uncle, Francis Radcliffe, had died after years of ill-health before the rebellion, in the summer of 1715, and Charles Radcliffe had, of course, lost his right of inheritance when attainted of high treason.

Charles Radcliffe lived in exile in extreme poverty until, in 1724, he

Charles Radcliffe, younger brother of the third Earl of Derwentwater married Lady Charlotte Mary Livingstone, Countess of Newburgh, and thereby acquired a considerable income. He spent the rest of his life living on the Continent with his family and upon his nephew's death inherited the title, fifth Earl of Derwentwater. Twice during this time he is thought to have returned to England, making an unsuccessful attempt to obtain a pardon, and it is said that on re-visiting Dilston he was mistaken for the ghost of his brother as he wandered in the woods around the Devil's Water.

In 1745 the second Jacobite Rebellion broke out and Charles Radcliffe, making his way by ship to join the rebels in Scotland under the banner of Bonnie Prince Charlie, was captured at sea and taken to the Tower of London. For a year he was kept in prison as no proof could be found of his true identify, and for a year he outwitted his enemies by pleading that he was a subject of France and held a commission from the French King. At his trial he displayed the arrogant defiance that was so typical of his fiery nature but he was eventually proved, partly by an old scar on his cheek, to be the same Charles Radcliffe that had escaped from Newgate and he was condemned to die by the sentence which had been passed upon him in 1716. Pleading his noble blood, he was allowed to undergo death by the axe, rather than by hanging, drawing and quartering, the original sentence.

On 8 December 1746 Charles Radcliffe, dressed very gaily in a scarlet regimental suit, brocaded waistcoat and white plumed hat, faced his executioners as bravely and proudly as James Radcliffe had done thirty years before. He was buried in St Giles-in-the-Fields and his heart was carried to Dilston by two loyal servants, where it was placed in a leaden box beside the coffin of his brother. Charles Radcliffe was the last Englishman to be executed in the Stuart cause and the last but one to die by the axe on Tower Hill.

Little has been written about the private life of Charles Radcliffe and even in the many and varied accounts of the Jacobite Rebellion his story is often sadly neglected. Charles Penrice, a writer who knew him well, describes him as:

Full of spirit and courage — bold and daring even to rashness, generally the first to offer himself to go upon the most hazardous enterprises. He seemed to set no value upon his life where honour was to be won, or service to be performed.

The writer goes on to describe some of the events during the march on Preston. He says that although Charles Radcliffe was far younger than most of the other leaders (being then twenty-two) he showed more capacity for command and greater strength of character than his more experienced companions. It was because of his fearlessness and bravery that the Earl gave him the command of his troops, and although Charles Radcliffe knew nothing of military discipline he inspired the men with great courage and confidence. 'During the whole action Mr. Radcliffe was in the midst of the fire, and exposed to as much danger as the meanest soldier then upon duty.'

Anya Seton, in her enthralling and well-researched historical novel, *Devil Water*, presents a remarkable account of the life of Charles Radcliffe based on a story that has been handed down in a Northumbrian branch of her family for generations. Family tradition claims that Charles Radcliffe, while still a youth, was kidnapped and forcibly married to a certain Meg Snowdon of Rothbury, after an amorous adventure which resulted in her pregnancy. The marriage was kept a strict secret in the Radcliffe family as it would have been a great embarrassment if it had become generally known. Charles was sent to London, where he acquired several mistresses and led a life of extravagance. He had the daughter of his concealed marriage removed from her rough moorland home and sent to London, where she was educated and brought up with the family of his cousin, Lady Betty Lee. Meg Snowdon died during Charles Radcliffe's exile and he shortly afterwards married the Countess of Newburgh. Charles Radcliffe was certainly the father of many illegitimate children, and this intriguing tale could explain why he did not officially marry until 1724.

Beside Langley Burn, near Haydon Bridge, is the Langley Cross, erected by the historian, Mr C. J. Bates, in 1883 when he bought Langley Castle, which was once a Derwentwater property, and restored it. The cross bears the inscription: 'To the memory of James and Charles, Earls of Derwentwater, Viscounts Langley, beheaded on Tower Hill, 24 February, 1716 and 8 December, 1746, for loyalty to their lawful sovereign'.

A verse (frequently recited by Samuel Johnson) portrays an accurate and vivid picture of this fascinating character:

> Radcliffe, unhappy in his crimes of youth
> Steady in what he still mistook for truth
> Beheld his death so decently unmoved
> The soft lamented, and the brave approved.

Adventurous, high-spirited, proud and courageous, he passed through his misguided days of youth and emerged as one of the bravest and most loyal supporters of the House of Stuart.

Sixteenth-century fireplace on first floor of Castle.

34

# 7. RELICS, REMAINS AND CURIOUS VISITORS

Over a period of several years, the management of the Dilston estates seems to have been badly neglected, for a large proportion of the furniture and Derwentwater belongings was taken by servants or given away as relics. Dilston Hall was taken over by several families who lived in it for many years until it fell into such disrepair that it was finally demolished in 1765. The Golden Lion public house in Corbridge, as well as several houses beside it, were built with stones from Dilston Hall.

Inside Alston Parish Church, restored and mounted, can be seen the single-pointer, seventeenth-century clock that once belonged to Dilston

Seventeenth-century clock from old Dilston Hall

Hall. The estates on Alston Moor, together with the rich lead mines, had belonged to the Radcliffe family since 1629 and it was decided by the Commissioners of Greenwich Hospital to present the clock and bell from the recently demolished mansion to Alston Parish Church. The bell has been there ever since and now forms part of a carillon of ten bells in the tower of the church. Unfortunately, the clock was damaged in its removal from Dilston and the face was lost. For two hundred years it lay neglected until, in 1977, the parishoners raised money for its repair and the construction of a new face of glass fibre.

A traditional story linked with Alston states that the Radcliffe family jewels were, at some stage, hidden inside the old hunting lodge there, but over the years the numerous attempts to find them have been in vain. Apparently the deeds state that, should the jewels ever be found, they must be shared with the Earl's heirs.

A house belonging to the Radcliffe family, on the west side of Newgate Street in Newcastle, was demolished in the mid-nineteenth century. The house had two stories, a garden, and a chapel with stained glass bearing the Radcliffe coat of arms.

The Derwentwater deeds and papers are kept in the Public Record Office, London. These papers were handed over to the authorities in 1746 when they were found hidden in three huge chests in a secret room under the roof of Capheaton Hall. They were discovered by a slater who recognized the Derwentwater coat of arms upon the chests. The documents had been hidden at Capheaton since 1715 when, during the last stages of the Battle of Preston, James Radcliffe, realizing that the rebellion was lost, had instructed his huntsman to take his horse and ride with haste to Dilston to secure the family deeds.

After the burial of James Radcliffe the family vault in Dilston Chapel was so disturbed by curious visitors that in 1775 orders were given for the entrance to be closed. But in 1805 the vault was officially re-opened, as doubt had been expressed as to whether the Earl's head had been buried with the body. It was found that both the body and the head had been embalmed and were in a state of complete preservation: the hair was perfect and the features regular and youthful. During this time, due to some carelessness and mismanagement, the vault was left open and several people took advantage of this to view the remains. One of them, a blacksmith, extracted several of the Earl's teeth and sold them for large sums of money. A local woman called Mrs Walters, who was at Dilston the day after the official opening of the coffin, claimed to have held the head in her hands and recalled that the features were perfect. Her companion, a young medical student, extracted a tooth and gave it to her, but the tooth was afterwards borrowed, to be used as a cure for

Interior of Dilston Chapel.

toothache, and was never returned. Mrs Walters described seeing a red moisture, which she called blood, following the extraction of the tooth, so that she had to wash her fingers in a pool of rain water close by.

In 1838 the vault was again opened and found to be in perfect condition. A small leaden box which had never before been noticed, was discovered and in it lay a human heart which was believed to have been that of Charles Radcliffe.

The Earl's coffin was removed in 1874 to Thorndon Hall in Essex, and placed in the family vault of Lord Petre, whose ancestor Robert James, the eighth Lord Petre, had married James Radcliffe's daughter, Anna Maria, in 1732. The other coffins were re-interred at the Catholic church in Hexham. These contained the remains of Francis Radcliffe, the first Earl who died in 1696; Edward Radcliffe, the second Earl who died in 1705; Mr Francis Radcliffe who died in 1704; and the Ladies Barbara and Mary Radcliffe who died in 1696 and 1724.

The clothes worn by the Earl on the day of his execution have been preserved by the Petre family, inside a mahogany chest. These scaffold clothes include a black beaver hat; coat, waistcoat and small clothes of black velvet; stockings that rolled to the knee; a wig of very fair hair that fell down on each side of the breast; a part of his shirt with the neck cut away; the black serge that covered the scaffold; and also a piece which covered the block, stiff with blood and with the marks of the axe in it. There is also a death mask modelled in alabaster. A certificate signed by Anne Petre the Earl's daughter attesting to the contents of the chest of clothes and requesting that the chest should never be used for any other purpose, is kept at the Essex Record Office and reads as follows:

I Anne, Lady Petre, widow of the Right Hon. Robert James Lord Petre, and only daughter and surviving child of James Earl of Derwentwater, who was beheaded in the year of our Lord one thousand seven hundred and sixteen, the twenty-fourth day of February, as by this writing testify, that all the wearing apparel in this mahogany chest was worn by the said James Earl of Derwentwater my father at the place of execution, and further that I, his above named daughter, out of the greatest respect, and veneration for my said father, caused this mahogany chest to be made on purpose to contain his said wearing apparel. But my principal motive in writing of this is to charge my son Robert Edward Lord Petre, who is likely to have this chest in his possession, and likewise my three daughters, Catherine, Barbara and Juliana should it ever come into theirs or into whose ever hand it should happen to fall, that they do not presume to apply this said chest to any other use, excepting only, that another chest or case more handsome should be provided to contain the said wearing apparel, my intention being that they should be kept with respect and veneration as is due to the memory of the said James Earl of Derwentwater.

In witness whereof I hereunto put my hand and seal this twelfth day of September, in the year of our Lord one thousand seven hundred and forty-eight.

ANNE PETRE

The scaffold clothes, the death mask and a portrait of James Radcliffe, third Earl of Derwentwater, can be seen at Ingatestone Hall, in Essex, the seat of the Petre family which is now open to the public. Also on exhibit are a number of items associated with the Earl as well as a portrait of his daughter, Anna Maria Petre, and a painting of Charles Radcliffe proposing to the Countess of Newburgh, after emerging from a chimney.

Unfortunately, other Derwentwater portraits and relics that were once kept at Slindon House, in Sussex, the home of Charles Radcliffe's descendants, appear to have been dispersed when the house and contents were sold in 1914.

The original letters written by James Radcliffe and Charles Radcliffe from the Tower, prior to their executions, are amongst a wealth of correspondence and papers relating to the Radcliffe family that have been deposited in the Essex Record Office in Chelmsford.

The vault at Thorndon Hall, containing the body of the Earl, has recently been badly vandalized and had to be restored and secured by local police. It is now in a private garden since Thorndon Hall, at one time the principal Petre family seat, has been turned into flats.

Death mask of James, third Earl of Derwentwater

# 8. THE DERWENTWATER ESTATES AND THE CRAZY CLAIMANT

The Radcliffes accumulated vast wealth from acquiring land by judicious marriage settlements over many years: they owned numerous estates and properties throughout Northumberland, Cumberland, Durham and Yorkshire. Sir Francis Radcliffe, the first baronet, his son Sir Edward, and Sir Francis, the third baronet and first Earl of Derwentwater, were all shrewd, hard-headed men who cleverly protected their gains during the persecution they suffered, as Catholics, in the seventeenth century. By the time that James Radcliffe inherited the Derwentwater estates, the Radcliffes were the richest Catholic family in the north-east. It was the fatal alliance with the Royal House of Stuart that eventually led to the ruin and extinction of this most ancient family, for when James Radcliffe and his brother Charles rode out to support their cousin, James Stuart, in the Jacobite Rebellion, the future of the family was sealed and the immense wealth that their ancestors had spent years accumulating was to be lost. During the following generations the male heirs of both James Radcliffe and Charles Radcliffe died young or without issue, and the Derwentwater estates, that had been confiscated by the government, were finally conferred upon Greenwich Hospital in 1735.

In 1833 John Grey, a Northumbrian landowner and progressive agriculturalist, was appointed by Greenwich Hospital as Receiver or land agent for the Derwentwater estates, and a new house was built for him at Dilston. This house is the present-day Dilston Hall and is situated not far from where the original building stood. Under the management of John Grey the revenue from the estates increased, though some properties were sold during this time. However, in 1865, following internal problems of administration at Greenwich Hospital, the Derwentwater estates were transferred to the Lords of the Admiralty.

In 1857, a woman calling herself Lady Matilda Mary Tudor Radcliffe laid claim to the Derwentwater estates. She professed to be the granddaughter of John Radcliffe, fourth Earl of Derwentwater, and supported this fantastic statement with a story that John Radcliffe had not died in 1731, but had gone to live in Paris where he had staged his own death, pretending to have died after a fall from his horse. There had already been attempts on his life organised by the Hanoverian government, and he had, therefore, decided that it would be wiser to

pretend to die. The self-styled Countess produced some dubious documents and had in her possession various relics, heirlooms, paintings and furniture which had belonged to the Radcliffe family or had, allegedly, come from Dilston Hall. After writing numerous letters to Lord Petre with her preposterous claim, to which she received no reply, she eventually turned up at Thorndon Hall, where she was given a cool reception. Failing to convince the Petre family of her supposed identity this determined woman moved north to live at Blaydon-on-Tyne where, in 1866, now calling herself Lady *Amelia* Mary Tudor Radcliffe, she told her story to the *Newcastle Weekly Chronicle*. For years she relentlessly carried on her campaign and in September 1868, together with two henchmen, she marched to Dilston where she set up residence in the ruined tower house, using a tarpaulin for a roof, hanging portraits on the walls and filling the place with pieces of furniture. She barricaded the door and stubbornly refused to move until, at last, she had to be forcibly carried out by a group of men. For several days she camped by the wayside at Dilston and caused a great sensation in the district. At first this eccentric, so-called Countess of Derwentwater received popular support, but eventually she was regarded as a fraud and thought to have spent years collecting her relics and heirlooms, studying the Derwentwater history at length and eventually fabricating her extraordinary story, probably even reaching the point where she believed it herself.

A few years later the Lords of the Admiralty sold off the remaining Derwentwater Estates to private owners. Dilston was bought by Mr W. B. Beaumont, the first Lord Allendale in 1874. Today the land beside the Devil's Water belongs to the present Lord Allendale and in the summer it is used as a camp site. Dilston Hall, the ruined castle and the chapel are the property of MENCAP, the Hall being used as a residential training unit.

# 9. FOR OWLS A DWELLING PLACE

Dilston Castle and Dilston Chapel are both Grade I listed buildings and scheduled ancient monuments, and are of exceptional importance. The Lord's Bridge over the Devil's Water, the arched gateway beside the Chapel and the gateposts at the entrance to the grounds, are listed as Grade II.

Dilston Chapel has belonged to the parish of Corbridge since 1733, when it was altered from a Roman Catholic chapel and re-furnished to suit the use of the Church of England. In 1874 it ceased to be used for worship but, in 1949, the Reverend Rex Malden, then Vicar of Corbridge, raised money for its restoration and it was re-dedicated for public worship that same year by the Bishop of Newcastle. A Corbridge parish document issued at this time describes the Chapel as being 'of quite exceptional historical and ecclesiological interest as being the only almost complete example of a private chapel of its period surviving in Northumberland and one of the very few in England'.

Dilston Castle was partially restored in 1910 by Lord Allendale but,

Dilston Castle and Chapel from the north-east.

42

Pathway through the river glen, below Dilston Castle, early in the nineteenth century

since then, it seems to have become regarded as a romantic but rather unimportant old ruin. Behind its crumbling walls and gaping windows only a first-floor level is still left intact and the stairway that led up to it from behind the door has partially collapsed. The interior, which is open to the sky, is increasingly threatened by encroaching trees and foliage.

To the north-east of the ruin and hidden high in the bankside is some interesting old stonework where the main block of the mansion house once stood. In the centre of this rubble is the entrance to an underground passage which leads off under the field in the direction of the ruin. Reference is made to this passage in *Dilston Hall* by William Sidney Gibson, published in 1850:

A low subterranean passage, which extends beneath the site of the demolished house, has been said to lead to a vaulted chamber beneath the ruins of this ancient tower — and it is said that there was a communication by a stair of many steps in a vaulted way, cut through the rock, from this chamber to the Divelswater, where there certainly are apertures in the rock that may have led to such a passage.

To the north of the ruin, over the bankside, it is still possible to walk down the old carriageway to the Lord's Bridge and the Devil's Water, though today the carriageway is no more than a rough track and the beautifully laid-out gardens, that stretched down to the river, are simply

Dilston Castle and Chapel.

a wilderness. The route of the old carriageway can be traced on the first Ordnance Survey Map of the area, printed in 1860, which shows that, after crossing the Lord's Bridge, it ran north-west, across the field beyond the river, and connected with the road to Dilston Mill. The water-mill, further downstream, dates back to the early fourteenth century and evidence of a medieval bridge was found in the river beside this spot.

The area beside the Devil's Water, which was once part of the ancient deer park, is wooded and very beautiful and, close to the Lord's Bridge, can be seen the remains of some ornamental stone walling, belonging to the formal, hanging gardens that feature in the old prints of Dilston Hall.

With a little imagination and the information available from books, prints, maps and plans it is possible to build up a picture of how Dilston used to be. The numerous stories and legends associated with James Radcliffe and these few, forgotten fragments of Derwentwater heritage are all that are left to remind us of the dramatic events that took place at Dilston so long ago. Without maintenance to ensure their preservation, even these relics could one day be lost forever.

These two views of the Devil's Water show the contrast between past and present. Although part of the old stone-walling, belonging to the stately gardens shown in the print, is still standing it is, sadly, beginning to collapse with the weight of trees

Underground tunnel amidst the rubble of what appears to have been part of the main block of the mansion. The tunnel was probably built at the same time as the house

This track, winding up from the river, is the route of the old carriageway from the Lord's Bridge to Dilston Hall. William Sidney Gibson, writing in 1850, describes the approach to Dilston Hall as first passing through an avenue of chestnut trees, then through a large gateway, after which the route wound round the hill near the river and bridge, before entering a formal and stately garden to the west of the mansion

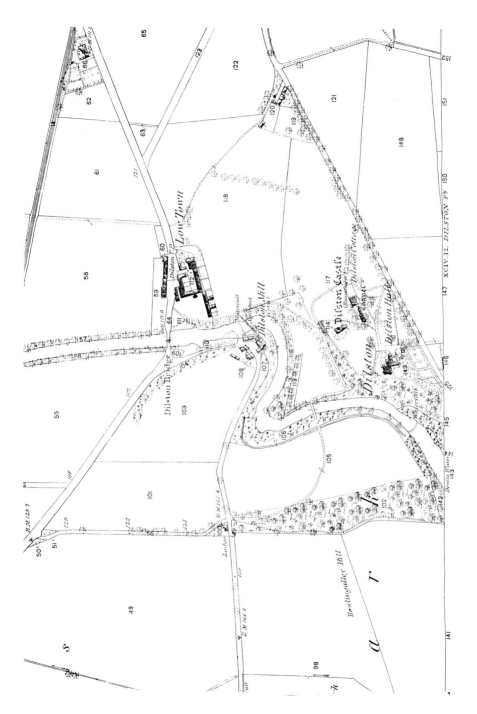

47

# BIBLIOGRAPHY

Arnold, Ralph, *Northern Lights*: The Story of Lord Derwentwater (1959)

Craser, H. H. E., *A History of Northumberland*, vol. 10 (1914)

Fisher Crosthwaite, J., *The Last of the Derwentwaters*: A paper read to The Keswick Literary Society (2 February 1874)

Gibson, William Sidney, *Dilston Hall* (1850)

Patten, The Reverend Robert, *The History of the Late Rebellion* (1717)

Penrice, Gerald, *A Genuine and Impartial Account of the Remarkable Life and Visissitudes of Fortune of Charles Radcliffe Esq* (1717)

Skeet, Major Francis John Angus, *The Life of the Right Honourable James Radcliffe, Third Earl of Derwentwater and the Life and Execution of his Brother Charles Radcliffe de jure Fifth Earl of Derwentwater* (1929)

Seton, Anya, *Devil Water* (1962)

Tomlinson, William Weaver, *Comprehensive Guide to the County of Northumberland* (1888)

*The Monthly Chronicle of North Country Lore and Legend*, vol. 4, nos 35, 36, 37 (1890)

*The Chapel of St Mary Magdalene, Dilston, Corbridge* Corbridge parish magazine 1949